AF409072

SINNER'S PRAYER

JASON MASINO

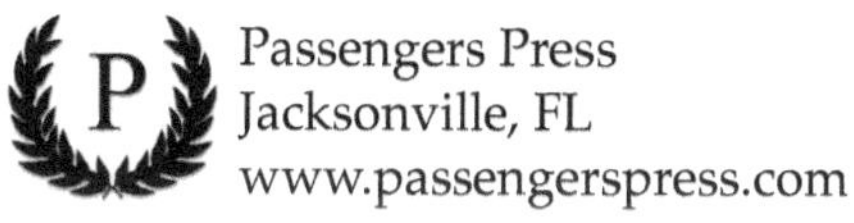

Passengers Press
Jacksonville, FL
www.passengerspress.com

Masino, Jason
1st edition.
ISBN: 979-8-218-11516-6

Manuscript Editor: Raphael Jenkins
Press Editor-in-Chief: Zac Furlough

Cover design and book layout: Andreea Ceplinschi
Author photo: Susannah McLeod (McLeod9 Creative)

Hear my sinner's prayer
I am what I am
And I don't wanna break the heart
of any other man
But you, but you

Hear my sinner's prayer
It's the only one I know
It sure as hell don't rhyme
But it's as good as, good as, good as, good as gold

-Stefani Joanne Angelina Germanotta-

I create this pain and anger on my own.

I try to be compassionate, tell my brain to shut the fuck up
& be grateful for what I have.

It never works.

Table of Sins

Gluttony

I'm not white, but growing up, Cindy Crawford and I had a lot in common

The Product

Think —

>
> Teddy Ruxpin
> meets
> Simon Says

Obey/er of three commands

- *Sit*
- *Here*
- *Stay*

Suggested wholesale: $39.99
Suggested retail: $69.99

the only way
this item will sell
is through a licensing deal

How to "make" a hu(man)

Oxygen	65 %
Carbon	18.5 %
Hydrogen	9.5 %
Nitrogen	3.2 %
Calcium	1.5 %
Phosphorus	1 %
Potassium	0.4 %
Sulfur	0.3 %
Sodium	0.2 %
Chlorine	0.2 %
Magnesium	0.1 %
Other[1]	< 1.0 %

---

[1] see *Inhumane*; see *<insert here>phobia*; see *Pillage*; see *Spoilage*; see *Type 2 Diabetes* with a side of (see) *Hypertension*; see *Gin & Tonic*; see *Antebellum South*; see *Poverty*; see *Two-Party System*; see *Double Quarter Pounder with Cheese*; see *Tyler Perry* (hates women); see *Eggnog*; see *Daytime Soap Operas*; see *Small Wonder*; see *Big Pharma*; see *Yourself*, and tell me what you see

Cheesecake Purse

This is something that Rachel would buy
If she didn't have one already
The first thing to show up is a selection from Etsy

Cheesecake purses - grab one here!

Canvas with strawberries and cheesecake printed on them
Purses that are shaped like actual cheesecakes
Held together by a golden chain
That is most likely plastic

& even though I can smell the purse
From my computer screen
I can't help but laugh
Because I'm pretty sure
Rachel already has one

& my mouth can't help but water
Because I can smell
& even taste it through my computer screen

Los Angeles

After Lisa Jarnot's *Sea Lyrics*

I am giving you life I am the chocolate in your peanut butter M&Ms I
am the smoke in your cigarette I am the smoke in your gun I am the gun
(*pow*) I am the sweat in your CrossFit I am the relaxation in your child's
pose I am the traffic I am the one who swiped left I am the one who cut
you off I am the smog I am the kelp in the ocean I am tired, but not as
tired as this city I am Los Angeles & I am killing you

Plastic fruit

If I could write you a song it would sound like
baby, baby, where did our love go?
I need to index these words before I'm gone

If my mind could speak/it would sound like lead
scratching on wood = paper crepes

Small waist, thick thighs/Ass don't sit as high/
Big feet, skeet-skeet/Complaining about the time;
if it's not used / is it stolen?

Come here, cinnamon, & honey buns
Bees swarming for that sweeeeeeet nectar
Marbled like a piece of chocolate meat

I know I shouldn't
but I dip the head of my cupcake
back into the funfetti frosting
And the $3.99 bar of Oregon's best white chocolate
And *2 for 1* Drumsticks

Looking for inspiration in iPod songs I keep on a loop
like fruit that nobody wants to eat
due to its manufactured plastic-y goodness

Greed

stick it in the mouth of the dead
and they'll spring right back to life

Autophobia

the specific phobia of isolation;
a morbid fear of being egotistical,
or a dread of being alone or isolated
        -Wikipedia

Ingredients

- The insides of a pig's stomach
- The insides of a robot's head
- The limbs of a wooden doll
- Contact lenses that should have been thrown out a long time ago

Prep

1. Preheat the oven to 350 degrees
2. Open the door
3. Stick your head in
    1. & give it a good sniff
1. Do not - I repeat - DO NOT REPEAT

The Goods

Lack of emotional control (-) too much student loan debt (+) do you have any friends? (-) stop talking to yourself (+) actually, it's not a bad thing/just don't let multiple voices in at once (+) just kidding - thinking you're crazy is just another form of being gaslit (x) how many friends do I have? (+) equal parts introversion and intuition (-) you're kinesthetically challenged (+) good grades don't mean shit if you don't know how to interact with people (/) without going crazy =

End Result

You're not crazy;
just socially-isolated

Hybridity Does Not Exist:
An Essay in Three Steps:

Step 1 — Ingredient Preparation — Unsuccessful Indoctrination

Hybridity Does Not Exist

The purpose of this essay is to make an attempt, but also speak to the idea of resistance. The resistance of definitive labels despite said labels being needed to define the self. And the resistance of writing a clean essay with a clearly defined beginning, middle, and end.

Another purpose of this essay is to survive. To make sense. To make real. To make true: of myself. The final and most important purpose of this essay is to posit that hybridity[2] is like an oxymoron and does not exist.

It is also important to note that despite oxymorons sometimes representing ineffectiveness, this essay liberally implores their use. A perfect example of this is the hybrid term "critical essay." On its own, an "essay" is a thought-out effort, so is not the "critique" implied? It is like a double positive, which is in the realm of a double negative, and as nonsensical as an oxymoron. Either way, the concept should not exist. Or this essay for that matter.

Let us preheat the oven and get started.

---

[2] For the sake of this essay, I will be referring to 'hybrid' as it relates to the evolutionary, which is general to the human condition and not specific to the literary; however, I reserve the right to pivot when necessary.

Step 1 — Ingredient Preparation — *Unsuccessful Indoctrination*

The overall feeling of growing up mixed-race is that you are neither here nor there. I grew up in the suburbs of Southern California and moved around much as a child. I constantly heard the phrase "no you're not" whenever I tried to define myself, particularly as black. What is funny is that, because I grew up in a lot of whiter areas and went to predominantly white schools, I was usually the "only…" in the room; however, until I was about five years old, I thought of myself as white. I remember running home one day asking Mom and Dad if I was white, and they laughed. Again, what is funny is that I never received a clear answer. Or maybe I did, of "mixed," but the memory is not quite there. This uncertainty has been reiterated as I have continued moving through life. I think it is because of what *white* meant to me.

As a 90s' child, growing up kind of poor and living near black and brown folks but going to school and having majority white friends, white was always *better*: better houses, name brands of almost any item versus generic brands, nannies to care for white kids at home instead of a television[3] set for the black and brown ones. White was also synonymous with "smarter," but this "white = smarter" myth was quickly dispelled for me.

In the first grade, I had a teacher who was not very good. During our math lesson, I would fail to grasp the concept as quickly as the other students. What I noticed was that they were repeating what she was saying rather than trying to find the answers via the typical mathematical steps. I did not have the language at the time to articulate that I thought she was a horrible teacher, so I stayed quiet, feeling stupid

---

[3] I find it funny that the word "television" — as American in concept as it is — is a hybrid of *tele-* from Greek and *vision* from Latin.

although I knew that I was not. The school assigned someone to test me and decided that I was "gifted" and placed me in the second-grade class. This is one of the few times in my life when I felt truly special.

And thus, my hubris was born.

However, I quickly learned that being "gifted" was akin to being cursed, especially if you did not know how to "properly" interact with people. I found that my newfound specialness was met with physical, verbal, and psychological abuse from everyone in my life, all in response to "getting smart" and "talking back," much like the force of a thunderbolt stricken by the gods:

> Of course the brown boy was punished so effectively that he does not remember the size, duration, or extent of the beating. And like all perfect traumas, the memory is recessed so deeply in the brown boy's brain that it may never surface. The memory, like the dumb cricket or other dumb bug, is dead[4]. (Wilson, 2008, p. 39)

I remember the '90s being very gendered, coming with an underlying rule that you must choose a side. But when you are open-minded and try to blend them both, you are chastised for not following a nonexistent script. I was always described as "pretty" versus "handsome" and loved to play with girly things; this supposedly should not exist for a boy.

This idea is best embodied by an experience from the second grade. When learning about the four primary colors (yellow, blue, red, and green), I remember asking the teacher, "What would happen if you blended them together — like a rainbow?" with childlike excitement. Another boy in my class, who was a new student in his first day, also

---

[4] Or, in other words, does not exist.

excitedly screamed "Yeah!" I remember getting in trouble over this for what seemed to be no reason. But in thinking about this experience over the years, it is clear that my proclivity to be creative was in direct opposition to the abovementioned nonexistent script. And my ability to rally additional troops landed me in the hot seat.

This color wheel story of mine is also symbolic of the idea that if you are not a typical boy you are slapped with the gay label — cultural suicide. Like rainbows, queerness already exists in nature, so it was like an extra denial of reality, my reality, and a denial of any of my intersecting black identity. This denial reiterated for me, as Joseph-Salisbury (2018) put it, "Black mixed-race men are simultaneously constituted by discourse and active in the constitution and recon-stitution of discourse" (p. 9).

As I moved into adolescence and my early teenage years, my queerness and blackness — two socially undesirable identities with equally violent slurs — forced me to become the butt of jokes, the source of threats and insults, forcing me to hate myself instead of being proud of these qualities:

> Faggot was a thought that snuck inside me, was put inside me, and all the fields inside me turned Greek, meaning tragic, meaning its beasts were hybrid and hard to slay: a faggot in the nigger, a nigger and a faggot and though both hollered I couldn't let them go. (Williams, 2016, p. 61)

Lust

the only thing sinister is the aftertaste

The Lesson

Winter, January XX, 2015

The first half of 2015 was filled with sex, drugs, and conversation. Trevor and I were still hanging out, smoking pot, and going at it like cats and rabbits. We hung out with each other many times during the week. The sex also got really weird, really quick.

A few years before, I bought a pair of Superman underwear with one of my friends. I was a different person back then and indulged in shopping with other gay dudes to please our boyfriends by wearing silly undergarments. I was too skinny but had nice legs. I looked and felt good.

Because of my voluntary unemployment situation, I was back at that weight. I had more time to do yoga and tone in my bedroom in the mornings. I was eating small amounts of food and was fitting into things I hadn't worn in years. I felt great, and like I was dying inside at the same time. I sometimes had a bottle of wine for dinner. I shaved all my body hair. I was a stone-cold mess.

One day, Trevor came over. I had on my Superman underwear. We had sex in my bed for the first time and it was fine. I didn't think about it much at the time, but he said something weird; that he was dirtier than he seemed and that "he'd done dirty, dirty things." I saw this as a challenge. I love challenges.

I took off my underwear and started to slap him in the face with it. He loved it. He called me "sir." I loved that.

"Do you like that?"

"Yes, sir."

"Are you a dirty whore?"

"Yes, sir."

Slap

"Thank you, sir."

I then stuffed my underwear in his mouth.

"Thank you, sir!"

"You're a filthy pig."

"Yes, I am, sir."

Slap

I'm hysterically laughing as I write this because I know how ridiculous it sounds. It's also extremely hot. We'd go at it for hours, and then his diabetes monitor would go off and he'd need to eat a protein bar or some Skittles.

Sometimes, not all the time, he'd come back to my place for a post-dinner smoke. One time before he left, I put my underwear in his briefcase. I told him to keep them in there and put his briefcase on his desk while he's teaching. He said, "This is a sick mind game, and I love it."

He was banging a lot of other dudes and I hated hearing about it. He didn't seem to catch on, so I passive-aggressively shut down and pretended like everything was fine. If we had another "date" set in stone, we were fine. But we weren't fine. I was a stone-cold jealous mess. I wanted him all to myself and he knew it. He liked the attention.

. . .

A lot of weirdness happened the following summer. My financial situation was bleak and I needed to get back to work. Trevor wasn't teaching much and had no reason to be in my neighborhood, so I didn't get to see him often.

This was around the time that Trevor and I stopped hanging out. He didn't really explain why, but hinted at having done "some really, really bad things." Intrigued, I assured him that he wasn't a bad person and that I'd still think highly of him, no matter what he'd done, but he refused to tell me anything.

I would've contested this but instead took it as a sign. I needed to get back into the groove of sitting on my ass all day and pretending to do meaningful work. I was smoking way too much weed and needed a tolerance break. I was putting on weight and was constantly bloated, probably from my many nights of getting super stoned and having a bottle of wine for dinner – red, not white. I was a stone-cold jealous trashy mess.

A few months later I heard from Trevor. He sent me a text asking me if I was alright, as someone we both knew died by suicide. His name was Jamie: he was gay, Filipino, and one of my closest friends. And quite possibly the sweetest person I'd ever met.

I knew Jamie from my undergraduate days when we were both theatre geeks. We didn't really hang out but saw each other in passing or at performances. It wasn't until some point in 2015 that we reconnected after learning we lived a few houses down from one another.

I knew Jamie was depressed but had no idea how severe his depression was. He used humor as an escape, which I practiced myself. Even sometimes I've used humor while writing to escape the pain of certain situations. The difference, though, is that I had experienced most of my hardship as a child, so my anger towards the world was my fuel and suicidal antidote. With Jamie, it was a slow and steady realization that the world wasn't built for people like us.

Jamie and I spent a lot of time together before he died. We hung out a few times a week, took the bus to work together, and constantly engaged in a role-play as two knockoff-Kardashian sisters that Kris Jenner didn't care for but felt obligated to include in the family because of our last name.

Jamie had a shit boyfriend – a white dude who didn't work. Jamie financially supported them both and gave him an allowance. One time, when Jamie went to the Philippines for a month, I caught his boyfriend on Grindr. They didn't have an open relationship. I never told Jamie.

None of our mutual friends knew Jamie's boyfriend, but the consensus was that we didn't like him. So, naturally, when it was reported that Jamie killed himself, no one believed it. I even called the police station and demanded they investigate his death more. Denial's a bitch.

I was visiting Southern California for a three-day weekend and told Jamie on the Friday of my trip. He seemed sad that I was leaving, but I told him that I'd be back by Monday. He died on Sunday. I was on the Amtrak and Trevor texted me right after someone else texted me about it. Trevor asked if I was alright and I told him that I never should've left for the weekend. He offered his condolences and that was it. I was a stone-cold jealous trashy mourning mess.

. . .

Buffy the Vampire Slayer aired from 1997 to 2003. *Buffy* follows the (mis)adventures of Buffy Summers, the blonde ex-cheerleader turned mythical Slayer equipped with superhuman strength, accelerated healing, and overall badass-ness. The dramedy, now a cult classic, was a balance of mythical-lore-meets-bird's-eye-view of a high schooler trying to live a normal life while battling vampires, demons, and other brutes.

At the beginning of season 3, a new slayer arrived in Sunnydale. Her name was Faith Lehane and she was quite literally the opposite of Buffy: dark eyes and features, angry, sexual, dangerous. No one knew why Faith showed up, which added to her mystique. But as the new toy, everyone was in awe of her and Buffy started to get jealous. Things got even more confusing when you found out why Faith was even there.

Faith had a watcher — aka: slayer mentor. Kakistos, a wrestler-looking vampire bro, killed Faith's watcher and made her watch. Faith badly wounded Kakistos but didn't kill him and left his face pretty messed up. She fled the scene and ran to Sunnydale, into the arms of Buffy.

By the time Buffy figured everything out and confronted Faith, they were greeted by Kakistos in a rampage of vengeance. They quickly found themselves in battle and Faith was unable to fight — she was stunned into submission. Kakistos promised to kill her like he did her watcher.

Buffy stepped into a mother-watcher role and tried to snap Faith out of her stupor. Faith never received formal training as a slayer, so Buffy offered sage advice: "The first rule of slaying: DON'T DIE." They ended up slaying Kakistos and calling it a night, but not before grabbing a bite to eat.

Although I'm a huge *Buffy* stan, Faith was my favorite slayer. Her enigmatic demigod-ness and dangerous yet charming style were fascinating.

. . .

I've always considered myself a caretaker, a skill that's followed me throughout early adulthood. I even had this energy with Jamie. He was a year or two older than I was, but I always acted like the older and more responsible sibling.

It took me a while to realize that I was living in a Buffy-fantasy but was more of a Faith type, which is probably why I was heavily drawn to her. In some ways, I did have it together more than Jamie. I coached him on almost everything and pushed him to do things he was scared to do. He was one of my closest friends, yet I feel like I barely knew him at the same time. He was enigmatic, charming, fascinating. And I was a tragic stone-cold jealous trashy mourning mess.

I have this irrational fear of falling to my death whenever I'm walking in the snow, in the rain, or home from a night of getting trashed at a local pub. Every few steps, I'll whisper to myself, "don't die!"

I wish I could've whispered that to Jamie the weekend he passed.

Jilted

The escape route:
- high on the sides
- sagging in the middle
- one stands to watch
    - as the other climbs out

I can't see past the bush you're hiding in;
a clear yet bordered view

- unresponsive
- unnerved
- smudged
- lightly stained

The silence of your sound lingers

…

…

…

you left the blinds open
for me to retrace your steps

Effed-up

Gun me down, gunner. Sufficiently awkward or is this a *new normal?* An invisible wall is up & between us; in the special space that I used to fill with my brown-boy-magic. The space that I swam in, that I teased in - trying to get to that sweet, gooey, sticky goodness in the middle. In the spot that I felt safe in: my room, my crawl space.

One man's fence is another man's moat, so I must ask: *can I dip my toes in the shallow end?* It's not exactly safe, so be on the watch and only let me drown if I need to.

I still want to venture into the deep end, both of us in shorts, leaving a hint of imagination and a splash of purgatory. I can work with the competing scents; the lack of cellular reception; the wooden diet; the vampire nightlife. Just give me the code and I'll open the locker myself.

I can get around by car, mind you. There just needs to be traffic cones and yellow tape. All you need is control board access, so let the boys have their cake.

Call me, Ishmael

Anchors aweigh! Thanks for accepting my proposal to the prom.
You brought me back to life, but as we know:
anything dead coming back to life hurts.

I'm in a crisis – *I need my mood to shift-shift back to good again.*
My unbridled passion, need for domination,
sharp teeth and chiseled nails - all yearn for symbiosis.
A true Herculean feat! Mount Mercurious is *my* bitch now.

Come hither and occupy the seat akin to my throne;
Take my spot if you so desire;
Swap out your prince's crown for my own;
Sit on my lap, or I on yours.

I threw a fistful of glitter into the air,
had the night's sky catch it and form our spirit animals:
these constellations I created for you:
a bear, a unicorn, cougars and lions, and whales, oh my!

Holy moly, fucking Moby and his dick & balls-!
Steep your candle with a tiny plate and put that fire out-
it seems to do nothing but get you into trouble

Anchors aweigh!

Set course to the east
Left is no longer, for I must do what is right

Endangered fishling:
I hereby release thee, back to Triton and his sea

What remains of me, you ask?

Let seagulls be seagulls, for bees will be free
Washed up from the ocean, my heart I can see

Hypnotize pt. 2

Sweet peaches move on two sticks, one by one

Let me lick the donut hole/
Glazed or plain/
Driving me to insanity and then…
sane

Eyes wide, I've finished/
Backing up, I want more/
but for now, it's my turn
Connect the mic, plug it in
Make me sing, baby, make me sing

Slender man with the slender hands
Can you do the can-can?
I'll join your band if you make me dance

Slather that heavenly breath all over me,
as you slide up and down my persona
Whispering in my ear about how
you're so proud of me

I forget all of my sources of tension/
Snort a few snorts, puff a few puffs

Ready, set, position!
Down on all fours or up on all three
I'm flexible, but only at the joints
Bend me into the shape
of your favorite color
and I'll happily oblige

Make me purr like a fucking kitty
Let my vocals fry as I moan, groan,
atone

But I'm not forgiven/
and neither are you/
So back to work, boo

My allure —
what would you describe it as?
And I ask you and your projections specifically because / as you say:

I'm just a catalyst.

A landmine
A distraction
A nuisance
A leech
A hobby
A meal & a snack, plus dessert
A nosebleed
A shot of whiskey
Or, just a friend,
just "someone you know"

Goodnight, Cheshire Cat!

The night's been wasted
Our bodies tasted
And smiles cast
on our wondrous faces

Amusing [mus{e}—ing, a] *adj.*

Like, when I laugh myself (temporarily) out of my depression comatose
— Or, when I sit alone at the bar / thoughts wavering behind my
increasingly blurring eyes — (Like), something like sarcasm after the
lady says *I'm Dutch* after my *I'm part-Indonesian* / before I say *Your people
colonized some of my people* and the room got quiet — Or, as I'm gazing
at nothing and you ask *Who's there?* and I say *Knock-Knock* — Like, up
against my walls as my glare tells you *Nobody's home* — Or, when a
musician stares at you while softly playing the drums and claims you as
his {muse} — Like the only black people in Disney's *Hercules* — Or,
when I confront you, and ask why you were staring; you guffaw *'Cause,
you're my muse* — Like, what I'm not after a corny joke — Or, the
electronic bass from *Seinfeld* — Like, the curvature of an apple-shaped
face behind raccoon eyes, a fire-beard, and the smell of burning wood
and soot through a modest *Chim chiminey Chim chim cher-oo!* and the luck
that shook off when we shook hands, too.

Passio

in my fake Chicago accent,
in your *good ol' Ohio*

> in my glass of whiskey,
> & the suffering stench
> caught in the air
> wafting slowly
> in y(our) direction

> > in the corner of the bar/
> > the corner of your lip,
> > sending silent smirks
> > down my shivering spine

> > in the cold,
> > secluded corner
> > out back/
> > pinch tobacco
> > <inside>
> > the middle of faulty paper;
> > smirk, lick, roll me a cigarette
> > & place it on my lips;
> > click-clack with your lighter
> > without my permission

> > clank-clank it
> > on my trolly
> > with a suffering spark;

> > close the fire
> > & call it a night

Apollo & Admetus

I wonder if
he's ever
~~killed~~ anybody

Answer to the question:
either *definitely* ~~or~~ *maybe*

He sticks his hands in his pockets,
sleeves over tatted sleeves,
no teardrops,
just a phone number

His pursed lips smite me
with the force of Zeus' bolt
on each cheek.

> *Make me an entry*
> *in your encyclopedia-*
>
> *give me definition*

Pride

I threw a fistful of glitter into the air

On Colonialism:

Don't try it - your sorcery won't work on me.
I stay open like a 7-Eleven on a Friday night.
Can't be fooled if I shoplift at my own store.
Are you mad that you can't make me your whore?

The oil wells below ground-zero are filled with my blood;
I was built to withstand, bear, enchant,
with just my hair, sweat, and musk in between.

My unpaid debt is my way of making a declaration
that this world is mine.
I promise you, I can't die.
Believe me, I've tried.

I scale through milky ways, seconds at a time,
examining the pool balls; fiddling and beating off to them,
just so I can leave my mark: I call them 'dangerous sparks.'

You can't beat *better* out of perfection -
the more you struggle, the harder I get.
I love a challenge as much as
I want your saliva, in my mouth,
so I can taste it, spit it out, then laugh in your face;
for effort, here's your 'A.'

Kanye West

Kanye West said it best
My hips don't lie but my ass does

Bask in my talents!
        Objectify me with your idealism
Fill me up with brass
        and I'll sing you some sugar
Play my body like a cello
        and I promise only sharp notes
        Unless you want them flat,
        like me,
        on my back

Jab me in the side with your stake
        & tear down these walls, Mr. Gorbachev!
Throw me against the wall like a crescendo
        & I'll lick the juice from your face once it splatters

But I won't clean up the mess

Why?

Because,

        Kanye West said it best

My Face | (see *Narcissism*)

It's hard to tell where my hairline ends and my forehead starts: I'm very wise, but no wrinkles live there. I obsessively stare in the mirror every morning, making sure that I don't have any hard lines - like a line break I didn't ask for. This is probably why I always have resting-bitch-face and never move it: if it doesn't move, it can't age.

Jumping off the cliff and landing onto my nose. There we have it: the trunk that was once too big for my tiny, skinny face. Up until high school, I was a stick and unable to gain any weight. This was probably because my nose stole it. It's the same size now as it was in the 7th grade when I had a weird growth spurt and became hairier and taller than all the other boys. They made fun of me, but they secretly wanted what I had. A bully used to take away my graphing calculator and would only give it back if I played with my facial hair. I thought it was bullying but realize now that it was foreplay.

At the bottom left, adjacent to my lip, lies a beauty mark. I'm not white, but growing up, Cindy Crawford and I had a lot in common. I've always been covered in them. When I was a kid, I was told that wherever on your body you had a beauty mark was beautiful.

Confession

I half/way atone for my sins

burned the village down
& started from the center

a Tasmanian-deviled spin
into the china shop

a parasitic seduction

a mocha stain on
your three-piece suit

Confidence

you want my intelligence with a side of submission
subtle feet/stubborn heat/assume the position
line up the slabs/piece by piece
obstructing my eyeline as I judge your person

Merlin & Pendragon have oh, so many plans for me
I'm Arthur-locked in my isolation tower
please, please let me be/leave me on the balcony
then, to the chimneys
shake up the crystal ball with me still inside
trying to pry with all of my might

might I borrow this light?
ignite the twine/blow me up & out
shoot through the roof and land on your plate
stand up and walk away
walk back into your room, point fingers at your face
my time, what a waste
turkey already stuffed, all I needed was a baste

The prickly plant devours its meal

pot o' gold at the end of the tunnel-
scale the walls, juice down my funnel-
pull up a chair-
hear my distant bellowing
as it slithers in your ears
smoother than a taint
act mad all you want
I humbly accept your thanks
lip smacker, back scratcher
saltine crackers
to soothe my upset tummy
mastication upon masturbation-
each releasing that *juice*;
nectar of deity, ambrosia;
stick it in the mouth of the dead
and they'll spring right back to life

Envy

Because I'm pretty sure
Rachel already has one
& my mouth can't help but water

Back to Black

Can you still shine bright
from six feet underground?

Culture transcends,
lives on
as the body - the bloody, soiled grape
prunes

Extract the soul and sell it
Ferment the insides and sell it

less than 2% remains as juice

Concentrate, can you?
See yourself, do you?

At what point
does a rant
turn into a plea?

What becomes of the body-
the bloody, soiled grape-
when history is wrung
from his skin?

Answerless questions
become obsessions
that I wish I had
the answers to

Questions that
mark a moment
on the analog;
a household's breath,
a whiff of oil frying on the stove,
of the Corn Man honking down the street

Don't all colors   add up to black?

Hypnotize pt. 1

Pied Piper, child catcher,
Hamelin's very own
1000 guilders - paid upfront

Charisma & followers,
mass musicious murderer,
irresponsible promises

Your creamy disposition shines the eyes,
my ever-purifying charcoal a contaminant

I stand on Saturn, you on Jupiter. Tell me -
if we were to crash, what would become of us?
Rings intertwined, gas, warm, hot, cold, smoke

These planets are the pool balls
and I am merely the table
on which we play

I'll just fade into…
perhaps the green, definitely the blue

Let's retrograde into Mercury;
no contracts, just a pinky promise
that you'll save a seat for me
somewhere on that spaceship

Chris Pratt [kriss-prat] *n.*

1. I had a dream that Chris Pratt was my annoying roommate and kept annoying me every second and said *if Wesley Snipes and I fucked and had a baby, it would look like you*; I said *that doesn't even make sense.* He then stole a few mini bags of M&Ms from me, even though I offered to give him some.

2. A few days later while binge-watching Top Chef, Chris Pratt and Anna Faris were guest judges. He made bad jokes the entire episode, and even his pseudo-authentic moments came off as annoying. The mediocre apple doesn't fall far from the proverbial white tree.

3. Chris Pratt is what happens when you're slightly good-looking and slightly funny and have a slight iota of talent. Chris Pratt looks like his dick smells funny. Chris Pratt had nice, thick legs and a firm ass in the first *Guardians of the Galaxy* film. Chris Pratt is living my dream life. Chris Pratt stole my job.

Hybridity Does Not Exist:
An Essay in Three Steps:

Step 2 — It's Time to Cook — What's for Dinner?

Step 2 — It's Time to Cook — *What's for Dinner?*

Beauty and intelligence are like a double-edged sword wielded by Apollo himself.

> His [Apollo] hair is smooth and made into tufts and curls that fall about his brow and hang before his face. His body is fair from head to foot, his limbs shine bright, his tongue gives oracles, and he is equally eloquent in prose or verse, propose which you will. What of his robes so fine in texture, so soft to the touch, aglow with purple? What of his lyre that flashes gold, gleams white with ivory, and shimmers with rainbow gems? What of his song, so cunning and so sweet? Nay, all these allurements suit with naught save luxury. To virtue they bring shame alone! (*Apuleius: Florida – Translation*, n.d.)

I spent ages 17 through 31 trapped in a college town, five years as an undergraduate and nearly ten as a contributing member of the capitalist machine, working for a large research university within the University of California system (the largest employer in the state). I liken the entire experience to the transition from a whole wheat or rye to a white bread. I erased my queerness and blackness to align myself with whiteness, which I saw as god-like, which granted me access to the finer things in life such as wealth, security, and comfort.

"Black mixed-race men also hold fluid and multiplicitous conceptions of self that allow them to engage in processes of hybridity in order to resist being torn asunder" (Joseph-Salisbury, 2018, p. 197). Unfortunately, this is not what happened.

I was suppressing power that I did not know existed. And like Africa, I felt exploited, abused, and appropriated for my natural resources. I was making good money, but not as much as I knew I was worth. My pay never decreased, yet my responsibilities did; I started in more strategic roles, and before I quit my cushy job my responsibilities included picking up trash and fetching breakfast burritos for my pregnant supervisor.

"but if a pimp is the god is the devil is the pimp is the dad is the pimp is the god is the devil" (Sikelianos, 2014, p. 13)

  … and I most certainly felt like I was pimped out and working for the devil. But unlike Buffy when she accidentally burned down her high school during battle after finding out she was a slayer ("Fandom," 2021), I intentionally set proverbial fire to the college town that had wronged me. And much like a hybrid, I was a symbiote that needed to get out from the oven that was baking, broiling, and overcooking me.

Sloth

If you don't speak it,
take the Latin quote
off your Grindr profile

Poet's Graveyard

Your inability
to use your imagination
          is gonna get you killed
          someday

I went through a goth phase in middle school

It's funny 'cause everyone said that it was a "white thing" but most of the people I went to middle school with were Mexican or Hispanic or Latinx so none of them were white. But a lot of them were goth, so that didn't make sense./I used to cry myself to sleep, praying to "god" to make the bullies stop./I went through a weird growth spurt in middle school. I grew a foot taller and became hairier than all the other boys. I was in the 6th or 7th grade/I became a goth so that people would fear me and leave me alone./It didn't work.

I used to be a poet | but now I am an observer

Merely a low tide, guided by the moon
A syncopated melody, a surprise
an interlude | an intro | an outro

If I stood on Pluto / would I cease to exist? A former shell of a
planet that's never made a full orbit — I look for inspiration in this
house of dead.

If I walked through a portal of time / would I break into fragments? I
close my eyes and wonder if the circle of life only happens on worlds
with an ecosystem.

I land on all four paws like a kitty. I burn my skin on the asphalt.

Is this alchemy?

Poured water at my feet and a pinch of charcoal on my forehead,
bread in my palms, and grains of sand stuck to my knees.

a.m. coffee

grind the beans in your head
& smell the aroma of morning

the best caffeine / is an internal mission
intention / is the best antidepressant
laughter, / the best core exercise
anxiety about the day, / the best laxative
your phone's alarm / is your puppeteer
& the notification of your account balance / is its master

but:

none of this is valid
        if you can't get out of bed

Heraclitus

A date with melancholy,
your misanthropic condition

Your religious ecstasy,
Dionysian lust,
oozing with serpent wine

Narcissus and his discus
stand proud
in the nude, like a statue
at full salute

Though fucked in your side,
I ask you to rise

For now, we sculpt in tandem
on these slick Grecian streets

I think I'm going to hell for not going to church

Mommy ran away from religion just to run back into it: we had a
two-year stint at a Catholic church that was in a small building one
year and a hotel banquet hall the other: there were free donuts: I was
baptized and confessed: it was weird and I don't believe in it: but I'm
still going to hell for not going to church.

Filtration

tainted water up the spout
through the faucet I fall out

to the land of busted glory
though without my native story

bees flocking to my nectar:
do they adore me,
or are they just boring?

teenage years
childish fears
catch my tears
please, stay here

screw the yellow hydrant back in—
contain the water
then, screw me
though I will not falter

Calgon

Take me to the backyard -
a hearty piss after diving in
12-feet deep / 12-song playlist
on the Memorex &
4 batteries and a floatie /
chlorine as the antidote to eczema

Take me to the deck-
newly built, freshly painted
2 boxes of Pizza Hut /
Lil' Kim & Ja Rule on the boombox,
Russian roulette
w/ a wet extension cord

Take me to the living room-
before the carpet was pulled up &
Coyote Ugly on VHS w/ a side of
Jasmine rice and fried shrimp /
ketchup / picante / & tartar sauce

Take me to the bedroom-
home alone w/ a bottle of Bacardi &
the boy from French class that I frenched
& claimed not to like /
played with the language of our tongues /
hickeys and cold silver spoons

Take me to the blueprint-
of this house I don't remember /
or the pools that touched my naked body &
siblings that are no longer mine but I miss /
& parents occupying their former shells

Take me up / and away
to the roof on proverbial fire /
& the back of a pickup truck /
cheap metal fences &

loose change stolen from the ashtray
in the middle of the night /
and barking dogs that know
not what they do or who they see

Ghosted

Casper is only friendly
when he texts back:

…

…

lack of stains
from fingerprints —

messy sheets
and a crooked pillow

Crooked (*adjective*)

like the pain in my neck

Crooked (*adjective*)

a con job

Infringe (*verb*)

on my 4th Amendment

a swab of spit;
a crispy crumb;
a trail that leads
to the start of my bedroom door

the only thing sinister
is the aftertaste

You left an impression on me

Pluto is no longer a planet/
   It was taken from me

I long for a simpler time/
   With similar rhymes

Roaches that hit the block/
   At 10 o'clock

Mamas yellin' for kids/
   To "come and get their supper"

Bellies tumbling in circles/
   Like linens in the dryer

Waiting

I waited at the top of the mountains. One of your mice asked about your being. I told him to get lost - *scram!* - go laugh to somebody else. I am not his keeper, so leave me with these peepers and let me bask in the neon lights.

I waited at the top of the mountains. My Cupid's Crown asked about your being. I told him to sit tight, Mighty Max. Endure the night & take flight when the time is just right. We are not his keeper, so let us leave him be with the other trees, for he is not to be kept with the bees.

I waited at the top of the mountains. Dandelion asked about your being. He told me that my thoughts were too loud - stay away from the clouds or I might fall down. I long to be your keeper but will leave you be as you cannot spell *free* without the extra *e*.

Hybridity Does Not Exist:
An Essay in Three Steps:
Step 3 — Time's Up! — Is there even anything on the plate?

Step 3 — Time's Up! — *Is there even anything on the plate?*

I am resisting the urge to continue in an autobiographical meets journal entry style and will instead venture back into the academic and scientific:

> Double consciousness is a fundamental component of Black mixed-race men's PRR[5]. An understanding of the threat one faces is essential to the cultivation of resilience. Contemporarily, this requires a rejection of the dominant ideology: the 'post-racial'. Double consciousness can inform one's sense of self… [and] can lead Black mixed-race men to hold multiplicitous and fluid post-racially resilient identities. (Joseph-Salisbury, 2018, p. 30)

In thinking of hybridity from an evolutionary perspective, a successful hybrid is considered a rare phenomenon (Seeker, 2015). About 200 years ago, Canadian farmers were worried about the potential extinction of wolves in the area. As more coyotes entered the forest, they began to breed with dogs and wolves due to the pressure put on them by the farmers. The result was a hybrid of all three animals, even though the distribution of genetics varied (65% coyote, 25% wolf, 10% dog); however, this newly created hybrid took the best traits equally from each of these animals. And while results are mixed, successful hybrid animals are defined by their resiliency (Seeker, 2015).

The world is built on cultural hybridity, but at the same time, it makes a conscious effort to deny it. This denial does not come only in the form of white people getting tans and brown people lightening

---

[5] Per Joseph-Salisbury, PRR is an acronym for *'post-racial' resilience.* 'Post-racial' is always within apostrophes suggesting that the concept does not really exist.

their skin, but also in the form of the dominant culture stealing from black and brown bodies and ideas and trying to pass them off as its own without giving proper credit (Newton, 2015).

Such as when the black community tried to generate "White Wealth" through Black Wall Street in 1921, "the type of community that African Americans are still, today, attempting to reclaim and rebuild" (Pickens, 2018). Or the $1.4 trillion "black spending power" (Repko, 2020) that does not seem to exist as the median salary of black people will be $0 by 2053 (Lartey, 2019).

It has become apparent to me that in my attempt to prove that hybridity does not exist, the departure of a hybrid autobiographical meets essay structure has caused me to psychologically unravel. And I also realize, ironically, that I have always considered myself a hybrid being, so does not that mean hybridity *does* exist? With that said:

I do not think I am any closer to figuring out
if hybridity truly does not exist
but it probably does not even matter
as I will not exist,
at least financially,
in twenty-two years.

Wrath

act mad all you want

Videre Possum

or, *I can see*

The disgust on your lip
the mustard on your toe
ketchup soaked in the bun
of your American hot dog

{*Videre possum*
or, I can see in Latin}

&, I can see the actual possum
climbing the electrical wires
in hopes for a snack of rat

a vicious reminder that I'm poor
in my own backyard

My lip quivers in disgust

Linguam Latinam loqueris?
[aka: *Do you speak the Latin Language?* in Latin]

If you don't speak it,
take the Latin quote
off your Grindr profile

My lip quivers in disgust
at your hubris

disgust at your American hotdog
ketchup soaked on your bun
mustard on your toe
disgust staring back at me

I'm a walking contradiction

I find myself walking up and down Colfax to let out my aggression. The homeless folks on the street never really bothered me, and kind of remind me of the streets of Downtown L.A.. I guess you can say it reminds me of home.

A million thoughts run through my mind when I strut down this busy street: why is the loudness so unpredictable, and why do so many people ride motorcycles? Is this a leftover product of the *good ol' cowboy days?*

Most of my pissiness comes from working as a federal volunteer with a shitty, measly monthly stipend. And how I'm a paycheck or two away from living on these streets as a beggar. How can I be "so smart" yet so unemployable at the same time?

A religious dude on YouTube talks about wrath being the embodiment of impatience, self-destructive behavior, and vengeance.

My mind goes back to the homeless people on the street. A woman screams to me: *sir, sir! Excuse me, sir!* I ignore her. I've seen her a few times, always pleading to folks walking down the street. She's in a wheelchair, and I think she has some kind of drug habit, but you can never be too sure. I worked for a homelessness nonprofit in Downtown L.A. and quickly learned that when it comes to folks experiencing homelessness, you can never pinpoint just one reason that led them there. But in my search for historical and political context, you quickly learn that it's a manufactured, deliberate system rooted in all kinds of shit from racism to classism — up, down & around, and back again. And let's not forget about our good friend Gentrification.

Money is power, and white people control wealth. Why are they always making it so hard for colored folks to bask in the fruits of their labor? Is it because of power? The religious YouTuber also talks about the concept of hate as wrath concealed. Do white people just intrinsically hate non-white people and take it out on them by restricting and blocking their access to wealth?

I think of my time working in business administration for California University, Dave's Ass. Where I wasted nearly 15 years of my life acquiring a so-called "top-tier" education and working my way up the career ladder. My knowledge and talents were feared, mainly by the whites that were double my age and twice+ my net worth. Their wrath concealed seeped through as passive aggressiveness and surface niceness coupled with backstabbing. I like to think of them as the X-Men Sentinel gatekeepers charged with maintaining the status quo and making sure I stayed in my low-paid place.

Fuck 'em.

Why haven't I gotten over this shit? I take a few deep breaths and remember that I need to breathe or I'll die prematurely, and that's akin to letting them win. Who the fuck is *them?*

I get closer to work, the government buildings on Broadway. This is usually my cue to get it together, work on faking a smile once I get into the building and pass by all the cops at the entrance near the metal detectors. I hate cops, but I'm pretty sure they know that. I'm one of the only brown things that enter the building not engaging in physical labor. Do they look at me, and my life that looks somewhat glamorous as I adorn myself in cute office attire, and think that I should be doing the boring shit *they* do?

I create this pain and anger on my own. I try to be compassionate, tell my brain to shut the fuck up & be grateful for what I have. It never works.

I wonder what Mrs. Dalloway would say.

Curious

Grab ahold of my hips
Bite and nibble on my nips
Enter this cave and rest, bitch
I keep a dollar worth in dimes
Don't keep track of the time
24/7 is the schedule I'm reppin'
Big things poppin'/like what you see, papa?
It's all yours baby
I've got more moves than a porn star but I'm not as classy
I'm nasty like a box of rancid candy, daddy
Rub on that spot with 4 fingers and a thumb
I can take it/better than the washers doing dishes
Unlimited capacity/no requirements other than awareness
And stupidness
And animal instincts
It stinks, huh?
I washed myself in a bath of my juices for you
Stick your tongue in and tell me how it tastes
I'm curious

Dianetics couldn't save us, even if it tried

Rachel and I couldn't help but laugh
during our tour of the L. Ron Hubbard Museum

Like you, Hubbard says to suppress the subconscious-
the "reactive mind"

Freud would argue that the "reactive mind"
is pretty much the id, drenched in pulp-science-fiction

I'm not a faggot; I'm just inspired by beauty

But, society says it's to be attributed
to my lack of a father figure
and my eternal daddy-search

Love your neighbor as you do thyself
or some shit like that

Why is this the book you believe in?

You do not love thyself
so you chose to take it out on me,
mongering tickets to the first row(s)
      at church
        no matter how many times
        I tell you that I don't want to go

Dianetics is like,
while conceptualizing psychoanalysis,
Freud took acid
      and fucked an alien
      on its spaceship
while Aristotle
and his cronies
      watched
in shock

and amazement
at its stupidity

This is the way
      I look at you
when you're leaving
the house
every Sunday morning

Run

Spring is in the air, bitches-! Run and hide!
The Sandman's out the bag/ready to make a catch
Mother earth and her hypocrite ways/created a mess to destroy itself
Starting with you/starting with me
She follows me during the day and lets me sleep at night;
permeating my thoughts/a bitter anxious aftertaste in the morning

She marks me with sweat whilst breathing down my neck/
Blowing a musky, stressful, blushing blow in my face/
Along with people-shaped rocks/and psychological air

My legs are dead so I can't run/I bathe in shit/sweat it out and drink it
Not fair-no one cares/unless you pay them in soul-colored dollars/
And even then, the heater doesn't work and you're stuck in the cold

I don't get it.

They see it and get hard/They want to lick it/
and stick their fingers in it/Taste the gold/
Mmm... you taste nice/Let's run it again

The devil comes (w/excuses)

He comes to flirt with me
But will never tell me
That he loves me

He'll cuff me tightly
But pledges his allegiance
Only to-

It's hot, isn't it?

This, he whispers
In the form of an emoji;
A winky-face, not an eggplant

Thirsty

Trickle-trickle
Down my legs
We're in a drought
Kipper and trout
Shut your mouth

You don't get to dictate anti-social norms
Your life remains a joke, wrapped in privilege,
sealed with my sticky, sloppy lips

The flames that once tortured my feet
Now is the fuel of my underlying desires
Brought to the forefront during games of footsies

You equal two of me, but I am much darker

Stronger
Able to weather the storm
And tame your bullish horns

But I'm not allowed to touch it
lest the Misses get involved

Use your whiskey-soaked dick
to fuck those bags of money
Then, me out of a seat

Sir Limp-in-the-Dick:
huff & puff the air
in & out of your chest
& blow these houses down

Your lungs haven't sung for their lives

a day in their life—
I toke, blow, with enough force to spare
Fumes permeating, mutating,
lost to a world of wonders

This is your first taste

My first rodeo
but not my first date

Weakest Link

Rx:

If

the kitchen is too hot,
you can't blame anyone
for your melting

you are margarine
you are shortening
you are ghee
you are curds & whey
you are spinning into butter

& your lies /
the enzymes

& what's left is
a penumbra
of a piñata

so-

if you're in the kitchen
& you think it's too hot

Then

step out of your hive
& show us what you've got

Acknowledgements

I want to thank Passengers Press for recognizing the specialness that is this book. I want to thank the good, the bad, and the ugly people that made this book happen.

And most importantly: this book is for the child that burned the village down.

Also:

1. "Autophobia" first appeared in Inverted Syntax (2020)
2. "How to "make" a hu(man)" first appeared in Obsidian: Literature & Arts in the African Diaspora, 48.2, 2022
3. "Back to Black" first appeared in its original form in Cultural Daily (2020)
4. "Effed-up" first appeared in Call + Response (2021)
5. "Amusing [mus{e}—ing, a] *adj.*" first appeared in Rigorous (2020)
6. "a.m. coffee" first appeared in Cultural Daily (2022)
7. "I used to be a poet | but now I am an observer" first appeared in Cultural Daily (2022)
8. "Filtration" first appeared in Squircle Line Press—Atelier of Healing: Poetry About Trauma and Recovery (2021)
9. "Calgon" first appeared in Rigorous (2020)
10. "Ghosted" first appeared in Quillkeepers Press—LGBTQ Pride Month Anthology (2021)

www.ingramcontent.com/pod-product-compliance
Lightning Source LLC
Chambersburg PA
CBHW020534160726